How to Reform
Capitalism

How to Reform Capitalism

The School of Life

Published in 2017 by The School of Life
70 Marchmont Street, London WC1N 1AB
Copyright © The School of Life 2017
Designed and typeset by Marcia Mihotich
Printed in Latvia by Livonia Print

A proportion of this book has appeared online at
thebookoflife.org

Every effort has been made to contact the copyright holders of
the material reproduced in this book. If any have been
inadvertently overlooked, the publisher will be pleased to make
restitution at the earliest opportunity.

The School of Life offers programmes, publications and
services to assist modern individuals in their quest to live more
engaged and meaningful lives. We've also developed a collection
of content-rich, design-led retail products to promote useful
insights and ideas from culture.

www.theschooloflife.com

ISBN 978-0-9957535-7-0

10 9 8 7 6 5 4 3

Contents

I
The *Nautilus* and Capitalism

Science fiction is one of the most popular but at the same time one of the least prestigious of the literary arts, frequently dismissed as a sub-genre consumed primarily by young males obsessed by the goriest or oddest possibilities for the future of our species.

Yet science fiction is a much-underestimated tool in business; in its utopian (as opposed to dystopian) versions, it invites us to explore imaginatively what we might want the future to be like – a little ahead of our practical abilities to mould it as we would wish.

Science fiction may not contain precise answers (how actually to make a jet-pack or a robot that loves us) but it encourages us in something that is logically prior to, and in its own way as important as, technological mastery: the identification of issues we would like to see solved. Changes in society and business seldom begin with actual inventions; they begin with acts of the imagination, with a sharpened sense of a need for something new, be this for an engine, a piece of legislation or a social movement. The details of change may eventually get worked out in laboratories, committee rooms and parliaments, but the crystallisation of the wish for change takes place at a prior stage, in the imaginations of people who know how to envisage what doesn't yet exist.

In his novel *Twenty Thousand Leagues Under the Sea*, published in Paris in 1870, Jules Verne (1828–1905) narrated the adventures of the *Nautilus*, a large submarine that tours the world's oceans often at great depth (the 20,000 leagues – about 80,000 kilometres – refer to the distance travelled). When writing the story, Verne didn't worry too much about solving every technical issue involved with undersea exploration: he was intent on pinning down capacities he felt it would one day be important to have. He described the *Nautilus* as being equipped with a huge window even though he had no idea how to make glass that could withstand immense barometric pressures. He imagined the vessel having a machine that could make seawater potable, although the science behind desalination was extremely primitive at the time. And he described the *Nautilus* as being powered by batteries – even though this technology was in its infancy.

Jules Verne was not an enemy of technology. He was deeply fascinated by practical problems. But in writing his novels, he held off from worrying too much about the 'how' questions. He wanted to picture the way things could be, while warding off – for a time – the many practical

Alphonse de Neuville and Edouard Riou, Illustrations for Jules Verne's

Twenty Thousand Leagues Under the Sea, 1871

'Wouldn't glass shatter at that pressure?'

Keeping certain questions at bay for long enough to shape a vision.

objections that would one day have to be addressed. He was thereby able to bring the idea of the submarine into the minds of millions while the technology slowly emerged that would allow the reality to take hold.

The key mental move in science fiction – 'what would we want life to be like one day?' – has traditionally been focused on technology. However, there is no reason why we would not perform equally dramatic thought-experiments in other fields, in relation to family life, relationships and, as we're about to do here, capitalism.

Asking oneself what a better version of something might be like, without direct tools for a fix to hand, can feel immature and naive. Yet it's by formulating visions of the future that we can more clearly start to define what might be wrong with what we have – and set the wheels of change in motion. Through science fiction experiments, we can get into the habit of counteracting detrimental tendencies to inhibit our thinking around wished-for scenarios that seem (in gloomy present moments at least) deeply unlikely. Such experiments are often hugely relevant, because when we look back in history we can see that so many machines, projects and ways of life that once appeared simply utopian have come to pass. Not least Captain Kirk's phone.

Captain Kirk's 'communicator' from Star Trek, 1966

Sometimes ideas drafted in science fiction pave the way

for real-life developments.

Changes in society and business seldom begin with actual inventions; they begin with acts of the imagination.

We all have a science fiction side to our brains, which we are normally careful to disguise for fear of humiliation. Yet, as Verne showed us, our visions are what carve out the space in which later developments can occur.

What follows is an attempt to work out aspects of a wiser future for capitalism.

2

Artists and Supermarket Tycoons

The Shanghai-based artist Xu Zhen (born 1977) is one of the most celebrated Chinese artists of our age. He operates in a variety of media, including video, sculpture and fine art. His work displays a deep interest in business; he appears at once charmed and horrified by commercial life. In recent years, he has become especially fascinated by supermarkets. He's interested, in part, in how lovely they can be.

Xu Zhen loves the alluring packaging, the abundance (the feel of lifting something off a shelf and seeing multiple versions of it waiting just behind) and the exquisite precision with which items are displayed. He particularly likes the claim of comprehensiveness that supermarkets implicitly make: the suggestion that they can, within their cavernous interiors, provide us with everything we could possibly need to thrive.

At the same time, Xu Zhen feels that there is something quite wrong with real supermarkets – and with commercial life in general. The products sold are rarely the things we genuinely need. Despite the enormous choice, what we require to thrive isn't on offer. Meanwhile, the backstories of the brightly coloured things on sale are often exploitative and dark. Everything has been carefully

Xu Zhen, *ShanghArt Supermarket* [Installation], 2007/2014

calculated to get us to spend more than we mean to. There's cynicism throughout the system.

In response, the Chinese artist mocks supermarkets repeatedly. His work involves recreating, at very large scale, entire supermarkets in galleries and museums. The products in these supermarkets look real; you're invited to pick them up, but then you find out they are empty, as physically empty as Xu Zhen feels they are spiritually incomplete. His checkouts are similarly deceptive. They seem genuine: you scan your products at a high-tech counter, but you then get a receipt that turns out to be a fake; you've bought nothing of value.

The supermarket installation takes us on a journey. At first it gets us to share the artist's excitement around supermarkets, then it punctures the illusion: it's a giant, deliberate let down. It's significant that Xu Zhen's critique of supermarkets is ironic. We tend to become ironic around things that we feel disappointed by but don't feel we'll ever be able to change. It's a manoeuvre of disappointment stoically handled.

A lot of art is ironic in its critiques of capitalism; we've come to expect this. It mocks all that is wrong but has no alternatives to put forward. A kind of hollow, sad laughter seems the only fitting response to the compromises of commercial life.

Xu Zhen is trapped in the paradigm of what an artist does. A real artist, we have come to suppose – and the current ideology of the art world insists – couldn't be enthusiastic about improving a supermarket. He or she could only mock from the sidelines. Nowadays, fortunately, we've loosened the restrictive definitions of what a 'real' man or a 'real' woman might be like, but there remain strict social taboos hemming in the idea of what a 'real' artist could be allowed to get up to. They can be as experimental and surprising as they like – unless they want to run a food shop or an airline or an energy corporation, at which point they cross a decisive boundary, fall from grace, lose their special status as artists and become the supposed polar opposites: mere business people.

We should take Xu Zhen seriously, perhaps more seriously than he takes himself. Beneath the irony, Xu Zhen has the ambition to discover what an ideal supermarket might be like, how it might be a successful business, and how capitalism could be reformed. Somewhere within his project, he carries a hope: that a corporation like a supermarket could be brought into line with the best values of art and assume psychological and spiritual importance inside the framework of commerce.

Thousands of miles away from Shanghai, in the flatlands of East Anglia in the northeastern tip of southern England, just outside of Norwich, lies an impressive modern building completed in 1978 by the architect Norman Foster. The Sainsbury Centre for Visual Arts is filled with some of the greatest works of contemporary art: here we find masterpieces by Henry Moore, Giacometti and Francis Bacon.

The collection is made possible thanks to the enormous wealth of the Sainsbury family, which owns and runs the large supermarket chain that bears its name. Discounted shoulders of lamb, white bread and 3-for-2 offers on tangerines have led to exquisite display cases containing Giacometti's elongated, haunting figures and Barbara Hepworth's hollowed-out ovaloids.

The gallery seems guided by values that are light years from any supermarket. It is intent on feeding the soul. The patrons and curators are deeply ambitious about the emotional and educational benefit of the experience:

The interior of the Sainsbury Centre for Visual Arts, Norwich.

they want you to come out cleansed and improved.

From a very different direction, the Sainsbury family arrive at a strikingly similar conclusion to Xu Zhen. Art and supermarkets are essentially opposed. Like Xu Zhen, the Sainsburys are caught in an identity trap, although a very different one: that of the philanthropist. The philanthropist has been imagined as a person who makes a lot of money in the brutish world of commerce, with all the normal expectations of maximising returns, squeezing wages and focusing on obvious opportunities – and then makes a clean break. In their spare hours, they can devote their wealth to projects that are profoundly non-commercial: the patient collection of Roman coins, Islamic vases or modern sculptures. But the philanthropist knows that if they ever took an art-loving attitude to their businesses they might suffer economic collapse. Instead of making big things happen in the real world, they would become mere artists who make interesting little things in the sheltered, subsidised world of the gallery.

The situation is strangely tantalising. The artist finds a little that is loveable and much that's wrong around supermarkets, but can't imagine running or bringing the ideals of art into action in one. The supermarket owners love art, but can't imagine bringing their psychologically and aesthetically ambitious sides into focus in their business. These two parties are both like pioneers, at the edges of unexplored territory. There is a huge idea they are both circling round. The goal is a synthesis of business and art: a supermarket that was truly guided by the ideals of art, a capitalism that could be compatible with the higher values of humanity.

Up to now, we have collectively learned to admire the values of the arts (which can be summed up as a devotion to truth, beauty and goodness) in the special arena of galleries. But their more important application is in the general, daily fabric of our lives – the area that is currently dominated by an often-depleted vision of commerce. It is a tragic polarisation: we encounter the values we need, but only in a rarefied setting, while we regard these values as alien to the circumstances in which we most need to meet them. For most of history, artists have laboured to render a few square inches of canvas utterly perfect or to chisel a single block of stone into its most expressive form. Traditionally, the most common size for a work of art was between three and six feet across. And while artists have articulated their visions across such expanses, the large-scale projects have been given over wholesale to businesses and governments – who have generally operated with much lower ambitions. We're so familiar with this polarisation, we regard it as if it were an inevitable fact of nature, rather than what it really is – a cultural and commercial failing.

Ideally, artists should absorb the best qualities of business and vice versa. Rather than seeing such qualities as opposed to what they stand for as artists or business people, they should see these as great enabling capacities, which help them fulfil their missions to the world. Xu Zhen will probably never get to build an airport, a marina, an old people's home or a supermarket, but the ideal next version of him will. We should want to simultaneously raise and combine the ambitions of artists (to make the noblest concepts powerful in our lives) and of business (to serve us successfully).

3
The Birth
of Consumer
Society

For most of history, the overwhelming majority of the world's inhabitants have owned more or less nothing: the clothes they stood up in, some bowls, a pot and a pan, perhaps a broom and, if things were going well, a few farming implements. Nations and peoples remained consistently poor: global GDP did not grow at all from year to year. Most of the world was as hard up in 1800 as it had been at the beginning of time. But then, starting in the early 18th century, in the countries of north western Europe, a remarkable phenomenon occurred: economies began to expand and wages to rise. Families who had never before had any money beyond what they needed to survive found they could go shopping for small luxuries: a comb or a mirror, a spare set of underwear, a pillow, some thicker boots or a towel. Their expenditure created a virtuous economic circle: the more they spent, the more businesses grew, and the more wages rose.

By the mid-18th century, observers recognised that they were living through a period of epochal change that historians have since described as the world's first 'consumer revolution'. In Britain, where the changes were most marked, enormous new industries sprang up to cater for the widespread demand for goods that had once been the preserve of the very rich. In England's cities, you could buy furniture from Chippendale, Hepplewhite and Sheraton; pottery from Wedgwood and Derby; cutlery from the smitheries of Sheffield; and hats, shoes and dresses featured in bestselling magazines like *The Gallery of Fashion* and *The Lady's Magazine*. Styles for clothes and hair, which had formerly gone unchanged for decades, now altered every year – often in extremely theatrical and impractical directions. In the early 1770s, there was a craze for decorated wigs so tall their tops could only be accessed by standing on a chair. It was fun for the cartoonists. So vivid and numerous were the consumer novelties that the austere Samuel Johnson (1709–1784), often referred to as Dr Johnson, wryly wondered whether prisoners were also soon 'to be hanged in a new way'.

The Christian church looked on and did not approve. Up and down England, clergymen delivered bitter sermons against the new materialism. Sons and daughters were to be kept away from shops; God would not look kindly on those who paid more attention to household decoration than to the state of their souls.

Along with the consumer revolution there also emerged an intellectual revolution that sharply altered the understanding of the role of 'vanities' in an economy.

Matthew Darly, *The Extravaganza; The Mountain Head Dress*, 1776

The motor of a sound economy: fripperies such as extraordinary wigs.

In 1723, a London physician called Bernard Mandeville (1670–1733) published an economic tract (unusually but charmingly written in verse) titled *The Fable of the Bees*. This proposed that – contrary to centuries of religious and moral thinking – what made countries rich (and therefore safe, honest, generous-spirited and strong) was a very minor, un-elevated and apparently undignified activity: shopping for pleasure. It was the consumption of what Mandeville called 'fripperies' – hats, bonnets, gloves, butter dishes, soup tureens, shoehorns and hairclips – that provided the engine for national prosperity and allowed the government to do in practice what the Church only knew how to sermonise about in theory: make a genuine difference to the lives of the weak and the poor. The only way to generate wealth, argued Mandeville, was to ensure high demand for absurd and unnecessary things. Of course, no one needed embroidered handbags, silk-lined slippers or ice-creams, but it was a blessing that they could be prompted by fashion to want them, for on the back of demand for such trifles, workshops could be built, apprentices trained and hospitals funded.

Rather than condemn recreational expenditures as Christian moralists had done, Mandeville celebrated them for their consequences. As Mandeville's subtitle put it, it was a case of: 'Private Vices, Public Benefits'. 'It is the sensual courtier who sets no limit to his luxury, the fickle strumpet who invents new fashions every week and the profuse rake and the lavish heir who most effectively help the poor,' he wrote. 'He that gives most trouble to thousands of his neighbours and invents the most operose manufactures is, right or wrong, the greatest friend to society. Mercers, upholsterers, tailors and many others would be starved in half a year's time if pride and luxury were at once to be banished from the nation'. Mandeville shocked his audience with the starkness of the choice he placed before them. A nation could either be very high-minded, spiritually elevated, intellectually refined, and dirt poor, or a slave to luxury and idle consumption, and very rich.

Mandeville's dark thesis went on to convince almost all the great Anglophone economists and political thinkers of the 18th century. In his essay *Of Luxury* (1752), the philosopher David Hume (1711–1776) repeated Mandeville's defence of an economy built on making and selling unnecessary things: 'In a nation, where there is no demand for superfluities, men sink into indolence, lose all enjoyment of life, and are useless to the public, which cannot maintain or support its fleets and armies'. The 'superfluities' were clearly silly, Hume was in no doubt, but they paved the way for something very important and grand: military and welfare spending.

There were some departures from the new economic orthodoxy. One of the most spirited and impassioned voices was that of Switzerland's greatest philosopher, Jean-Jacques Rousseau (1712–1778). Shocked by the impact of the consumer revolution on the manners and atmosphere of his native Geneva, Rousseau called for a return to a simpler, older way of life of the sort he had experienced in Alpine villages or read about in travellers' accounts of the native tribes of North America. In the remote corners of Appenzell or the vast forests of Missouri, there was, blessedly, no concern for fashion and no one-upmanship around hair extensions.

Rousseau recommended closing Geneva's borders and imposing crippling taxes on luxury goods so that people's energies could be redirected towards non-material values. He looked back with fondness to the austere martial spirit of Sparta and complained, partly with Mandeville and Hume in mind: 'Ancient treatises of politics continually made mention of morals and virtue; ours speak of nothing but commerce and money.' However, even if Rousseau disagreed with Hume and Mandeville, he did not seek to deny the basic premise behind their analyses: it truly appeared to be a choice between decadent consumption and wealth on the one hand, and virtuous restraint and poverty on the other. It was simply that Rousseau, unusually, preferred virtue to wealth.

The parameters of this debate have continued to dominate economic thinking ever since. We re-encounter them in ideological arguments between capitalists and communists and free marketeers and environmentalists. But for most of us, the debate is no longer pertinent. We simply accept that we will live in consumer economies with some very unfortunate side effects (crass advertising, unhealthy foodstuffs, products that are disconnected from any reasonable assessment of our needs) in exchange for economic growth and high employment. We have chosen wealth over virtue.

An irony-laden acceptance of this dichotomy is what underpinned the approach of many Pop artists of mid-20th-century America. Claes Oldenburg (born 1929) developed a reputation for taking modest consumer items, many of them food-related, and reproducing them as large scale soft vinyl forms. In galleries typically devoted to high art where one would have expected to find oil paintings and marble sculptures, one now came across an outsized hamburger, a giant slab of cake or a huge plate of fries decked with ketchup. In the mid-70s, Oldenburg began a long and productive partnership with Dutch/American writer and art historian Coosje van Bruggen (1942–2009). They too worked on a grand scale – installing huge steel and aluminium outdoor sculptures in university grounds, plazas and parks. One of their most famous collaborations continued the fascination with fast food – a 12-metre-high stainless steel ice cream cone, upturned on a shopping mall on the corner of the busy Neumarkt Square in Cologne, a city whose skyline is filled with conical church spires.

Oldenburg's vast versions of small things playfully direct our attention to the peculiar dependence of modern economies on the mass consumption of what are, in human terms, some deeply negligible products. Yet the scale of Oldenburg's works is only superficially absurd, for it rather precisely reflects their central importance in our collective economic destinies. Nevertheless, as Oldenburg seemed to concede, it was peculiar to be living in a civilization founded on the back of buns and sweetened tomato paste – a bathos hinted at by

Claes Oldenburg and Coosje van Bruggen, *Dropped Cone*, 2001

the deflated, detumescent appearance of the giant comestibles that feature throughout his work.

The one question that has rarely been asked is whether there might be a way to attenuate the dispiriting choice, to draw on the best aspects of consumerism on the one hand and high-mindedness on the other without suffering their worst sides – moral decadence and profound poverty. Might it be possible for a society to develop that allows for consumer spending (and therefore provides employment and welfare), yet of a kind directed at something other than 'vanities' and 'superfluities'? Might we shop for something other than nonsense? In other words, might we have wealth and (a degree of) virtue?

It is this possibility of which we find some intriguing hints in the work of Adam Smith (1723–1790), an economist too often read as a blunt apologist for all aspects of consumer society, but in fact one of its more subtle and visionary analysts. In his book *The Wealth of Nations* (1776), Smith seems at points willing to concede to key aspects of Mandeville's argument: consumer societies do help the poor by providing employment based around satisfying what are often rather sub-optimal purchases. Smith was as ready as other Anglophone economists to mock the triviality of some consumer choices, while admiring their consequences. All those embroidered lace handkerchiefs, jewelled snuff-boxes and miniature temples made of cream for dessert were flippant, he conceded, but they encouraged trade, created employment and generated immense wealth – and could be defended on this score.

However, Smith held out some fascinating hopes for the future. He pointed out that consumption did not invariably have to involve the trading of frivolous things. He had seen the expansion of the Edinburgh book trade and knew how large a market higher education might become. He understood how much wealth was being accumulated through the construction of Edinburgh's extremely handsome and noble New Town. He understood that humans have many 'higher' needs that require a lot of labour, intelligence and work to fulfil, but that lie outside of capitalist enterprise as conceived of by 'realists' such as Hume or Mandeville: among these, our need for education, for self-understanding, for beautiful cities and for rewarding social lives. The ultimate goal of capitalism was to tackle 'happiness' in all its complexities, psychological as opposed to merely material.

The capitalism of our times still has not entirely managed

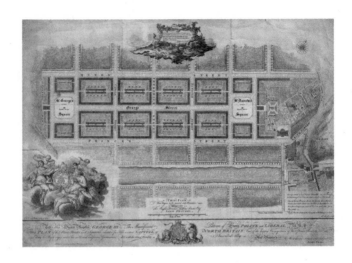

James Craig, *Plan for Edinburgh New Town*, 1768

A promise of noble consumption.

to resolve the awkward choices that Mandeville and Rousseau circled. But the crucial hope for the future is that we may not forever need to be making money off exploitative or vain consumer appetite; we may also learn to generate sizeable profits from helping people – as consumers and producers – in the truly important and ambitious aspects of their lives. The reform of capitalism hinges on an odd-sounding, but critical task: a conception of an economy focused around higher needs.

4

Higher Needs, a Pyramid and Capitalism

The idea that capitalism can give us what we need has always been central to its defence. More efficiently than any other system, capitalism has, in theory, been able to identify what we're lacking and deliver it to us with unparalleled efficiency. Capitalism is the most skilled machine we have ever constructed for satiating human needs.

Because businesses have been so extraordinarily productive over the last 200 years, it has become easy to think – in the wealthier parts of the world, at least – that consumer capitalism must by now have reached a stage of exhausted stagnant maturity, which may explain both relatively high rates of unemployment and low levels of growth. The heroic period of development, driven in part by breakthroughs in technology, that equipped a mass public in the advanced nations with the basics of food, shelter, hygiene and entertainment, appears to have been brought up against some natural limits. We seem to be in the strange position of having too much of everything: shoes, dishcloths, televisions, chocolates, woollen hats.... In the eyes of some, it is normal that we should have arrived at this end-point. The planet and its resources are limited, so we should not expect growth to be unlimited. Flat-lining reflects the attainment of an enviable degree of maturity. We are ceasing to buy quite so much for an understandable reason: we have all we need.

Yet, despite its evident successes, consumer capitalism cannot realistically be credited with having fulfilled a mission of accurately satiating our needs, because of one evident failing: we aren't happy. Indeed, most of us are, a good deal of the time, properly at sea: burdened by complaints, unfulfilled hopes, barely formulated longings, restlessness, anger and grief – little of which our plethora of shops and services appear remotely equipped to address. Given the range of our outstanding needs and capitalism's theoretical commitment to fulfilling them, it would be profoundly paradoxical to count the economy as in any way mature and beyond expansion. Far from it; it is arguably a good deal too small and desperately undeveloped in relation to what we would truly want from it, once we reflect on the full extent of our sorrows and appetites. Despite all the factories, the concrete, the highways and the logistics chains, consumer capitalism has – arguably – not even properly started on its tasks. A good future may depend not on minimising consumer capitalism but on radically extending its reach and depth, via a slightly unfamiliar route: a close study of our unattended needs.

A good future may depend not on minimising consumer capitalism but on radically extending its reach and depth.

If a proverbial Martian were to attempt to guess what human beings required in order to be satisfied by scanning lists of the top corporations in the leading wealthy countries, they would guess that *homo sapiens* had immense requirements for food, warmth, shelter, credit, insurance, missiles, packets of data, strips of cotton or wool to wrap around their limbs and, of course, a lot of ketchup. This, the world's bourses seem to tell us, is what human satisfaction is made up of.

But the reality is more complicated. The most concise yet penetrating picture of human needs ever drawn up was the work of the American psychologist Abraham Maslow (1908–1970). In a paper titled 'A Theory of Human Motivation' published in *Psychological Review* in 1943, Maslow arranged our longings and appetites on a pyramid-shaped continuum, ranging from what he called the lower needs, largely focused on the body, to the higher needs, largely focused on the psyche, and encompassing such elements as the need for status, recognition and friendship. At the apex stood the need for a complete development of our potential of a kind Maslow had seen in the lives of the cultural figures he most admired: Montaigne, Voltaire, Goethe, Tolstoy and Freud.

The pyramid of our needs according to American

psychologist Abraham Maslow.

If we were to align the world's largest corporations with the pyramid, we would find that the needs to which they cater are overwhelmingly those at the bottom of the pyramid. Our most successful businesses are those that aim to satisfy our physical and simpler psychological selves: they operate in oil and gas, mining, construction, agriculture, pharmaceuticals, electronics, telecommunications, insurance, banking and light entertainment.

What's surprising is how unambitious consumer capitalism has, until now, been about many of the things that deliver higher sorts of satisfaction. Business has helped us to be warm, safe and distracted. It has been markedly indifferent to our flourishing.

This is the task ahead of us. The true destiny of, and millennial opportunity for, consumer capitalism, is to travel up the pyramid, to generate ever more of its profits from the satisfaction of the full range of 'higher needs' that currently lie outside the realm of industrialisation and commodification.

Capitalists and companies are seemingly – at least semi-consciously – aware of their failure to engage with many of the elements at the top of the pyramid, including friendship, belonging, meaningfulness and a sense of agency and autonomy. Evidence for this lies in one of the key institutions for driving the sales of capitalism's products: advertising.

5

The Promises
of Advertising

When advertising began in a significant way in the early 19th century, it was a relatively straightforward business. It showed you a product, told you what it did, where you could get it, and what it cost.

Then, in 1960s America, a remarkable new way of advertising emerged, led by Madison Avenue luminaries such as William Bernbach, David Ogilvy and Mary Wells Lawrence. In their work for brands like Esso, Avis and Life Cereal, adverts ceased to be in a narrow sense about the things they were selling. The focus of an ad might ostensibly be on a car, but our attention was also directed at the harmonious, handsome couple holding hands beside it. It might on the surface be an advert about soap, but the true emphasis was on the state of calm that accompanied the ablutions. It might be whisky one was being invited to drink, but it was the attitude of resoluteness and resilience on display that provided the compelling focal point. Madison Avenue had made an extraordinary discovery: however appealing a product might be, there were many other things that were likely to be even more appealing to customers; by entwining their products with these ingredients, sales could be transformed.

Patek Philippe is one of the giants of the global watchmaking industry. Since 1996, they have been running a distinctive series of adverts featuring parents and children. It is almost impossible not to have glimpsed one somewhere.

In one example, a father and son are together in a motorboat, a scene that tenderly evokes filial and paternal loyalty and love. The son is listening carefully while his kindly dad tells him about aspects of seafaring. We can imagine the boy will grow up confident and independent – yet also respectful and warm. He'll be keen to follow in his father's footsteps and emulate his best sides. The father has put a lot of work into the relationship (one senses they've been out on the water a number of times) and now the love is being properly paid back. The advertisement understands our deepest hopes around our children. It is moving because what it depicts is so hard to find in real life. We are often brought to tears not so much by what we have as by what we long for but cannot reach.

Father–son relations tend to be highly ambivalent. Despite a lot of effort, there can be extensive feelings of neglect, rebellion and, on both sides, bitterness. Capitalism doesn't allow dads to be too present. There

Patek Philippe advertise their watches with an appeal to

our real longing: family happiness.

It is love we want; it is Calvin Klein we buy.

may not be too much chance to talk. But in the world of Patek Philippe, we glimpse a psychological paradise.

We turn to Calvin Klein. Here the parents and children have tumbled together in a happy heap. There is laughter; everyone can be silly together, there is no need to put up a front, because everyone is trusting and on the same side. No one understands you like these people do. In the anonymous airport lounge, in the lonely hotel room, you'll think back to this cosy group and ache. Alternatively, you might already long for those years, quite a way back, when it was so much easier than it's become. Now the kids are shadowy presences around the house. Your relationship with your spouse has suffered too. Calvin Klein knows this; it too has brilliantly latched on to our deepest and most elusive inner longings.

Adverts wouldn't work if they didn't operate with a very good understanding of what our real needs are; what we truly require to be happy. Their emotional pull is based on knowing us eerily well. As they recognise, we are creatures who hunger for good family relationships, connections with others, a sense of freedom and joy, a promise of self-development, dignity, calm and the feeling that we are respected.

Yet, armed with this knowledge, they – and the corporations who bankroll them – are unwittingly cruel to us. While they excite us with reminders of our buried longings, they cannot do anything wholehearted about quenching them. Adverts may want to sell us things, but these are incommensurate things in relation to the hopes that they have aroused. Calvin Klein makes lovely cologne. Patek Philippe's watches are reliable and beautiful agents of time-keeping. But these items cannot help us secure the goods our unconscious believed were on offer.

The real crisis of capitalism is that product development lags so far behind the best insights of advertising. Since the 1960s, advertising has worked out just how much we need help with the true challenges of life. It has fathomed how deeply we want to have better careers, stronger relationships, and greater confidence. In most adverts, the pain and the hope of our lives have been superbly identified, but the products are almost comically at odds with the problems at hand. Advertisers are hardly to blame. They are, in fact, the victims of an extraordinary problem of modern capitalism. While we have so many complex needs, we have nothing better to offer ourselves than, perhaps, a slightly more accurate timepiece or more subtly blended perfume. Business needs to become more ambitious in the creation of new kinds of 'products', in their own way as strange-sounding today as a wrist watch would have seemed to observers in 1500. We need the drive of commerce to get behind filling the world – and our lives – with goods that can really help us to thrive, flourish, find contentment and manage our relationships well.

To trace the future shape of capitalism, we only have to think of all the needs we have that currently lie outside of commerce. We need help in forming cohesive, interesting, benevolent communities. We need help in bringing up children. We need help in calming down at key moments (the cost of our high anxiety and rage is appalling in aggregate). We require immense assistance in discovering our real talents in the workplace and in understanding where we can best deploy them. We have aesthetic desires that we can't seem to get satisfied at scale, especially in relation to housing.

Our higher needs are not trivial or minor wants; insignificant things we could easily survive without. They are, in many ways, central to our lives. We have simply accepted, without adequate protest, that there is nothing business could do to address them, when being able to

To trace the future shape of capitalism, we only have to think of all the needs we have that currently lie outside of commerce.

structure businesses around these needs would be the commercial equivalent of the discovery of steam power or the invention of the electric light bulb.

We don't know, today, quite what the businesses of the future will look like, just as half a century ago no one could describe the corporate essence of the current large technology companies. But we can know the direction we need to head to: one where the drive and inventiveness of capitalism tackle the higher, deeper problems of life. This will offer an exit from the failings that attend business today. In the ideal future for consumer capitalism, our materialism would be refined, our work would be rendered more meaningful and our profits more honourable.

Advertising has at least done us the great service of hinting at the future shape of the economy; it already trades on all the right ingredients. The challenge now is to narrow the gap between the fantasies being offered and what we spend our lives making and our money buying.

6

The Depression
of the Business
Community

Throughout history, when business has been harshly judged, criticism has focused on the idea of greed; business is bad because it is an activity driven by greed.

However, this badly misses the point. If one were to accuse business of any single flaw, it should not be greed but *pessimism*. Business has been surprisingly pessimistic about how money can be made. Hard-headed managers have rarely been outright corrupt or unnaturally avaricious: but they have very often suffered from a curious kind of melancholy, a distinctive sadness about the world and its inhabitants. This sadness shows itself in six major assumptions that operate beneath the workings of modern business:

1. Customers will never care about workers

A great many businesses employ the very cheapest labour they are able to locate on the planet. They negotiate contracts that mean that millions of people have to work in dangerous or at least uncomfortable factories and warehouses until their premature deaths.

It is tempting to assume that pure nastiness drives these mean-minded decisions: employers must be screwing their workers because they are greedy. But the truth is far stranger: they are pessimistic and uncreative about the mindsets of their customers.

Capitalists have a primordial need to stay in business and must be ready to do whatever is compatible with this aim. If it turned out that paying staff extremely well was in line with this ambition, they would do so at once without rancour or qualm.

They don't, because they have made some dark assumptions about these customers. They are bleakly sure that few customers will ever care much about the wellbeing of workers; they won't give a damn how many eight-year-olds are making their trousers or how much suffering went into harvesting their tea leaves – and therefore, for businesses to start caring about such issues will simply lead to a decimation in profits.

It is not a personal longing on the part of businesses to have people work for as little as possible. The low salaries stem from the assumption that unless businesses stick to rock-bottom wages, customers will go elsewhere and their enterprises will fail.

2. Customers have low appetites that can't be improved

There is a deep belief in many areas of business that high-mindedness, sincerity and complexity are fatal to sales and that any attempt to 'raise' the aspirations of consumers in these directions is guaranteed to lose money.

There is, for example, rampant pessimism around what would happen if you used less salt in a restaurant, or made certain magazines a little more thoughtful or produced a car that was gentle on its surroundings. As the business community is fond of rehearsing: no one ever failed to make money underestimating the tastes of the public.

3. The only way to sell is through deception

There is a painful background belief that in order to thrive, a business must make enormous claims for its products, and ideally create semi-conscious associations between what is sold and success, fun, love and sex.

The people behind adverts don't themselves believe that buying a certain perfume, car or phone will be closely connected to physical intimacy or popularity. But they are confronted with some gloomy facts about human nature: that people do seem to buy such items if you skilfully make airy promises about them.

Few businesses can possibly believe that advertising in its current state is admirable. If they resort to it, it is just from a desolate conclusion seemingly drawn from experience. A company can of course choose to be above such things but sales will fall, profits will drop, salaries will be cut; they won't be able to raise capital and the whole venture will eventually fold. You can participate in a charade – or you can be poor.

4. You can only make big money from the bottom of the pyramid

As we have established, most of the big and most profitable corporations on the planet address needs grouped at the lower levels of Maslow's pyramid. These businesses efficiently target the basic needs: for shelter, security, communication and energy. They are engaged in real estate, mining, oil, insurance or transport. None of these industries are currently focused in any ambitious way on what happens around their products. The oil company doesn't care much what your journey is about, so long as you travel a lot; the real estate corporation isn't concerned with the kind of life you live in your apartment, so long as you pay the rent.

It's not that people in business don't care about meaning, creativity and the pursuit of self-knowledge. It's just that they have a pessimistic conviction that it is impossible to make money from concerns that will always remain elusive and private.

5. You can't afford to care about the psychology of your staff

This is no reflection of personal indifference to the inner lives of others; it's just (many in business will feel) a crucial fact about running an enterprise: if you start getting concerned about the people who work in an organisation, focus will be taken away from the harsh task of turning a profit. Then it won't matter how kindly you feel towards your people, as you won't be able to give them the one thing they actually want from you: a job. Business requires the softer or more generous aspects of one's nature to be held in check.

6. The only legitimate role for surplus wealth is philanthropic donation

Successful capitalists can be extremely generous. The arts have been noted beneficiaries of their largesse; scientific organisations too. Yet the area that tends not to benefit so much is the core activity: the profitable business itself. This is generally run with extreme rigour and no eye towards the finer, more meaningful, element. The higher things are what you commune with on the weekend and give away money to on your retirement; they can't be part of your core activity. You squeeze margins, shave quality and bat away riskier projects for 40 years, and only then help to fund the opera house.

It is these pessimistic ideas about commerce and work that lead many companies – and the people who run them – to make very poor decisions. What is really at play is a pained vision of life in which any higher aspiration seems condemned to failure.

The big claim here is that this pessimism is not always warranted; and that in order to overcome it, business should look to an unusual source for inspiration: culture. It is culture that possesses a welter of antidotes to much of the underlying despair about humanity evident in commerce.

If this antidote has never been explored, it's because business understandably has some deep suspicions of its own when it comes to culture. The whole field seems negligible. When you look at what really counts in the world, none of it seems to have much to do with culture. The big corporations are concerned about millions of things – drilling rights, exchange rates, employment laws, tax credits, regional instability, technological advances. Culture appears marginal to this. It is just an upmarket area of entertainment; a hobby. You might know of a CEO who paints watercolours to relax, or a wealthy family that subsidises a ballet company. This is delightful, but it shows where the arts fit in – you become involved in the arts once you have made money. The arts use up money; they don't make it. In essence, for business, culture looks like something you might become interested in once you have succeeded, but it can't help you to succeed.

But in this arena too, there has been excessive pessimism. There's a way of considering culture that brings out a hitherto unexplored and highly intriguing set of ideas for business. With the right mindset, we can go through the six pessimistic assumptions, one by one, and see alternative – and more optimistic – attitudes that might be available through the history and practice of culture:

1. We care about those we can imagine

Art is ambitious about the possibility of creating emotional connections between strangers. The basis of many artistic works has been the desire to generate sympathy where none initially existed. A central skill of art is to guide us to perceive a common humanity where at first there was anonymity and otherness. In her novel *Middlemarch*, Mary Ann Evans (1819–1880), who published as 'George Eliot', was concerned with teasing out the hidden dignity and honour of people living unglamorous lives: a small-scale builder, a modest farmer, a carpenter, a servant, a poor clergyman. She made large numbers of readers feel kindly and concerned about these characters; she added new regions to our maps of sympathy.

Her technique did not involve telling her readers they ought to care. She didn't scold. She described people's lives carefully, feeling that the more we know about others, the more we will feel for them. She was deeply against overt didacticism and lecturing about the plight of the poor. Eliot's style was 'psychological realism'; she gave her readers a sense of what it was to be other people, and then let readers come to their own conclusions – which they have been doing successfully for over a hundred years.

George Eliot may be one of the most famous writers in the world's most influential language, but she remains a very small deal in a noisy, distracted planet. Nevertheless, her example justifies a degree of confidence that wider sympathy can be engaged; a sympathy for bricklayers and surveyors, but also garment makers, tea leaf pickers, fast-food workers and (in case we were to forget) bankers and CEOs. The pessimistic view that customers are only selfish – and can never care about the workforce, and so will never bear the costs connected with care, is not true to the emotional mechanics of culture.

2. Taste can vary immensely

The idea that companies should give people what they currently want is a guiding principle of business. But the bigger facts of culture show just how flexible, surprising and fast-moving changes in taste can be.

In 18th century Britain, members of the same species as we belong to today became interested on a large scale in poetry. Alexander Pope (1688–1744), the leading poet of the day, introduced the twelve-syllable hexameter (against the advice of many) and was convinced that consumers would be highly sensitive to its rhythms. He was right. People loved the slightly slower pace and the neater rhymes it made possible – and he was able to buy himself a magnificent villa, just outside London, on the proceeds.

The raking of gravel is not something that, at present, seems like a major human concern. But in Japan, over many centuries, people became interested in the patterns into which gravel could be arranged in even very small gardens. Getting it right was hugely important to them. They also became very aware of the different characteristics of moss and the best ways of grouping rocks together. It's evidence of how – with the right encouragement – enormous groups of people can become highly sensitive to features that, in other societies, go entirely unnoticed.

These cultural instances reveal a fundamental fact about how the whole basis of our excitement can shift. Taste is a variable factor. We're good at appreciating moves of taste in retrospect. It's in advance that we are much less alive to the phenomenon. Therefore, businesses routinely end up assuming that their customers can't care about anything that goes too strongly against what currently exists.

Culture should embolden business. Until around 1919 no one had really thought that you could like a painting that didn't try to represent anything. Then came Piet Mondrian (1872–1944), who avoided painting trees or sunsets or mothers and babies so as to focus our attention more clearly on distinctive abstract qualities: harmony, balance and purity. Mondrian shook off a depressed sense that preferences are fixed. He approached public taste with a justified optimism that, in principle, and with

79

Piet Mondrian, *Composition with Yellow, Blue and Red*, 1937–42

a bit of time and support, many people can be brought to recognise the appeal of novel and interesting things. It worked. A modest Mondrian now costs the price of a medium-sized jet.

If the expansion of taste works in relation to lines on a canvas, it must work in other, far more important, areas than art: the immensely significant realms of food, cars, hydroelectric turbines, data storage and clothing.

3. Goodness can be advertised

Business is familiar with the idea of seduction, but it takes a limited view of where seduction can be usefully deployed. For its part, culture has also been interested in charm, but it has used it far more ambitiously: to try to 'sell' difficult and higher things.

The Ancient Greeks, for instance, often presented rationality (the potentially austere demand that we think carefully and logically) via the god Apollo. But they knew that in order to get their ideas across, they would have to make Apollo attractive. So in a lot of their art, he looks like a cross between a model and a football player, his hair always a tumble of locks, his forearms strong.

François Girardon, *Apollo Attended by the Nymphs of Thetis*

(copy of Greek original), c. 1666–73

A classical advert – for wisdom.

The optimistic assumption was that we can be enticed towards elevated, noble or serious tasks with the help of the right sensory associations, if they are introduced in a sufficiently alluring way. The very techniques that could be used to sell bullshit can also be deployed to sell wisdom and self-understanding.

4. Important sensations can be commodified

Culture addresses the top level of Maslow's pyramid of needs: it is concerned with the pursuit of meaning and the exploration of individuality and freedom. At certain important moments, it has also succeeded in commodifying experiences in these areas and turning them into very profitable commercial operations.

Impressionism – one of the most commercially successful ventures of all time (if it was a stock, it would be near the very top of most exchanges) – began when a group of painters living and working around Paris in the 1860s became entranced by the play of light on the top of clouds, the delicate tones of shadows in city streets, and the shimmering reflection of sunshine on water. They had had really lovely experiences walking by rivers, strolling through gardens and picnicking in woodland.

The largely deserted, rugged coast of Normandy was visited by Claude Monet (1840–1926). He was particularly attracted to the cliffs near the village of Etretat. Many local people and one or two rare visitors must occasionally have had the fleeting thought that it was a charming place as they drew up a fishing boat on the sand or collected the iodine-rich kelp.

The difference with Monet is that he took the pleasure of looking at the cliffs very seriously. He painted a series of works closely examining how beautiful the light could be at different times of day and studied the pattern of shadows on the rocks.

His paintings kick-started Normandy's tourism business, now one of the most important in France. The pessimistic idea that big profits cluster around lower needs isn't justified. Billions of dollars of value can be created out of people's interest in how a cliff can look after a heavy spring shower.

5. People will do more or less anything for you, if the purpose feels high enough

The pessimistic idea is that people only work for money.

Claude Monet, *The Cliffs at Etretat*, 1885

Yet across history, we see people – often celebrated in art – touched by other significant motivating ambitions to make the highest sacrifices.

The medieval monks who designed and constructed the buildings on the Scottish island of Iona did not have competitive salary packages. They worked because they were motivated by an idea that had been compellingly presented to them: that their labour would be pleasing to God.

Revolutionaries have regularly sacrificed their lives not because they were going to be paid to liberate a building, but because they were drawn to the idea of serving their country, even this were to come at a terrible personal price.

Churches and revolutions don't have a natural monopoly on the optimistic idea that people can be driven by things other than merely money; these are just a couple of areas in which proponents happened to have been particularly ambitious. Many corporations in fact serve the public good in important, if less overtly dramatic, ways. They too can benefit from our striking disinterest in money when meaning is on offer.

Across history, we see people touched by other significant motivating ambitions to make the highest sacrifices.

6. The true destination of art is outside the museum

We see how often surplus wealth goes into art, and art is surely a deserving recipient. But even more valuable are the sorts of things that works of art celebrate: kindness, empathy, goodness, beauty and meaning.

In the utopia, the qualities found in art would not remain in art. They would have more of a place in our daily lives, and especially in our offices and factories. The true desire of artists has never been just to make art; it has been to transform the world in line with the ideas housed (temporarily) in art. It is surely closer to the true spirit of art to run a business that properly enhances our lives – even at the cost of reducing rates of profit – than to over-promote, make false promises or cut corners for decades and then give a Renoir to the National Gallery. The world's museums would certainly be less well endowed if the world's entrepreneurs had not accumulated vast fortunes. The world's houses and shops would probably look a lot more beautiful and therefore more loyal to the aspirations of culture if entrepreneurs accepted a more modest rate of return on their investments in exchange for decent-looking, noble products.

What we've been seeing via culture is a set of reasons to be less pessimistic about business. An incidental skill of culture emerges: to correct the more melancholy accounts of how money can be made. It can do this by identifying a range of skills and ideas around inner life, communication, how to change people's minds and the role of higher needs that have real impact on business itself. Because we meet with certain ideas in culture, it is a ready assumption to think that they belong in culture alone. But culture is only a modest outlet for big capacities that deserve to exist far more widely and in a far more important arena: that of business.

7

The Future
of Brands

High-minded people are often instinctively suspicious of the idea of brands. Brands can seem hateful on many grounds: their maddening ubiquity (they surprise us on a mountain walk or on arrival in a new country where we'd gone specifically to experience a different culture); they squeeze out smaller independent alternatives to which they are often inferior; or they radiate values that appear to us fake, exaggerated or plain daft. It is natural to suppose that we would, ideally, live in an unbranded world.

It is not surprising we feel this way. There are, after all, a lot of bad brands around. Nevertheless, something important remains submerged within the essential concept of a brand. A good economy should not be one devoid of brands; it would be one with better brands.

In a narrow sense, a brand is a visual cue that declares the origins of a product or service. More broadly, it alludes to the underlying character or personality of a company. Brands present, in highly condensed forms, encompassing visions of what life might be about. So beguiling might these be that our desire to make a purchase can originate not so much in a desire for a particular product or service as in a wish to tie ourselves more closely to the philosophies that hover over them.

Furthermore, brands usher in expectations of coherence and consistency. We expect that – under the umbrella of a brand – very similar things will happen across countries, employees and products. Brands allow qualities and ideas to multiply powerfully across the world.

This is the problem, for brands threaten to repeat idiocy on an industrial scale wherever they spread. However, with perspective, we can see that the true culprit is never the pure fact of repetition. The objection is to what is being repeated.

In the 16th century, the Italian architect, Andrea Palladio (1508–1580) worked out a set of basic designs for villas, churches and public buildings, based on a set of ideas assembled from Roman and, to a lesser extent, Greek architecture. He built his first versions in the little town of Vicenza. But his views spread rapidly, first across the Veneto, then more broadly through northern Italy, France, England, Germany, Russia and – especially – the United States. With a few concessions to local materials and colours, more or less identical buildings appeared in St Petersburg and Edinburgh, Boston and Berlin. Libraries, palaces, schools and homes acquired an astonishing basic consistency of appearance. Palladio's

Thomas Jefferson, Monticello, Virginia, built 1772.
Jefferson's aesthetic borrowed heavily from the 'brand' of architecture developed by Palladio.

highly readable architectural manual, *I Quattro Libri dell'
Architettura* ('The Four Books of Architecture', Venice,
1570) detailed how to lay out rooms, organise façades and
treat window decorations, and became an indispensable
part of every architect's library in the West. In America,
Thomas Jefferson (1743–1826) was the great defender of
this Palladian brand. His own house at Monticello and the
campus of the University of Virginia were key examples of
a franchise architecture that became no less widespread or
well known than that of roadside McDonald's restaurants
two centuries later.

That we might not lament the ubiquity of Palladianism
as much as the omnipresence of fast-food restaurants
suggests that the issue with brands isn't really about
repetition, but about the repetition of mediocrity. In
fact, the potential of brands to repeat good things is
central to what we should respect about them. Although
our societies may be highly primed to respect individual
genius, progress in many areas is dependent on an ability
to institutionalise the insights of geniuses, codifying their
moves and distilling and teaching their methods.

A good brand performs a critical function in this regard:
it can compensate society for the rarity of talent. It

may enable the ideas of one especially clever person to influence how half the world will look. As a result of brands, geniuses will not always be directly needed to bring about something of genius – which is important, given how few geniuses tend to be around. Brands move the focus away from individuals towards the collective, attempting to insulate quality from the chance feelings or attitudes of a lone creator. Brands ensure that the good need not always be unique.

To date, the idea of collecting great talent under a brand has found its most developed form in art. Titian (c.1488/1490–1576) was one of the most prolific artists in 16th century Venice, but he also understood early on in his career that he would never be able to deliver personally all the many commissions he received. He therefore set up a large studio in which he employed a troop of highly talented artists – among them his nephew Marco and his brother Francesco – whose style became almost indistinguishable from his. The master's name would guarantee the quality of the object – but it would not necessarily have hovered too much over any one particular canvas. Lute players, landscapes and Madonnas that would otherwise have struggled to come into being emerged from the studio for the churches and palaces of Europe under a coherent Titian brand.

Brands almost invariably have logos. These too have a bad name. We accuse them of spoiling views, degrading the skyline and getting in the way. However, the issue is once again less with logos in their essence than with particular logos – and they might make up a majority – that come with unfortunate associations. Yet at a theoretical level, a logo simply possesses an important power to focus our minds almost instantaneously on qualities we can expect of a location or object that carries it. So attuned are our eyes to drawing out the meaning of shapes and colours that talented graphic artists can hope to inscribe highly nuanced philosophies of life fairly accurately into the smallest visual cues. The Christian lamb, or *Agnus Dei*, has been one of the most successful of all logos, appearing on stained-glass windows, the sides of pulpits, tunics, plates or weather vanes, and condensing the spirit of the entire Gospels into a single redolent image.

We should not aim to eliminate brands and their logos, but to grow more ambitious about what a global brand might be capable of. For example, it is a pity that the British child psychoanalyst Donald Winnicott (1896–1971) remains just one individual who produced a few

William Warrington, Agnus Dei stained glass window

Field Dalling, Norfolk, 1856

This 'logo' has been used to transmit the spirit of the Gospels in

one condensed image.

immensely wise books and lectures that colour the education of some present-day analysts rather than, as should have happened, a brand that kept certain of Winnicott's lessons permanently in our minds, through the use of buildings, education programmes, films, a clear ideology – and a good logo.

Winnicott stood for close bonds between parents and children, a gracious acceptance of our psychological eccentricities, a wise accommodation with what is 'good enough' in life, work and love, and a recognition of the importance of games and toys (especially teddy bears) in the emotional development of children. These values could, in the hands of a talented graphic designer, find themselves distilled into a logo that would, when glimpsed on the city skyline or the side of a domestic object, trigger a rehearsal of a crucial set of ideas and embed these more securely in our fragile and forgetful minds.

A morally neutral approach to business defines a 'good brand' as one that is popular and well known. It is impressed by how many people recognise a logo. But we should be raising a different set of criteria for the value of a brand. A good brand is one built round a set of genuine virtues: of qualities properly anchored in a capacity to help us develop flourishing lives.

Brands invite the recognition that great things are not usually done by individuals acting in heroic isolation. The hallmark of a thriving culture is not, in fact, the dominance of the lone celebrity; it is the dominance of brands. Brands rescue good things from the cult of individualism, which, though flattering, sets us up with a big collective problem, for it denies the good the chance to be active in a widespread way. At some point, every decent idea and every important insight should go through the process of becoming a brand and thereby gain from a huge extension of its reach. The world is in sore need of better brands.

8
The Future
of Selling

New York's Times Square pays mesmerising tribute to the power of selling. Seen at night on foot, one can't fail to be awed by the quantity of effort and ambition focused here. The entire square and (it feels) the sky glow with the longing to persuade and seduce – in the name of a watch or a hamburger. It is easy to feel scornful.

Chartres Cathedral was built between 1194 and 1250. It too was a giant exercise in light and colour dedicated to selling. We may think that selling is at the root of modern problems, but it's the selling of low ambitions that is the true cause. The north transept rose window of Chartres Cathedral is ten metres in diameter and is one of the crowning glories of Western culture. In a central oculus shine Mary and Jesus, surrounded by twelve diamond-shaped windows containing the kings of Judah. In five lancet windows beneath, morality tales from the Old Testament are illuminated in vivid purples, yellows and blues: in one, Aaron triumphs over Pharaoh, warning us of the need to live godly, observant lives.

Chartres is selling as well: just at a more profound level. Its sponsoring organisation was a corporation trading in ideas concerning forgiveness, love, duty and kindness. It wasn't doing this simply in order to make money; these

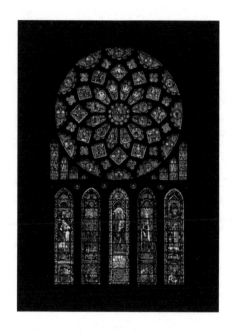

North window transept of Chartres Cathedral.

This stunning artistic accomplishment 'sells' the highest Christian values.

were its foundational convictions.

The difference between Times Square and Chartres Cathedral isn't to do with selling; it's to do with ambition. We remain at the dawn of capitalism. We can imagine a Times Square of the future dedicated to the promotion of cures for loneliness, aids to forgiveness and those psychological ingredients that will help us be wise and kind.

We don't have to stop selling: we need to learn to engage commercially with our highest needs.

p.80
Composition with Yellow, Blue and Red,
1937–42, Piet Mondran
Photo: © Tate, London 2017

p.82
Apollo Attended by the
Nymphs of Thetis,
c. 1666–73, François Girardon
Photo: Flickr / Daniel Jolivet / CC
BY 2.0

p.85
The Cliffs at Etretat, 1885, Claude
Monet
Photo: Art Collection 3 / Alamy
Stock Photo

p.95
Photo: Martin Falbisoner /
CC BY 3.0

p.99
Agnus Dei, Lamb of God, stained
glass window by William
Warrington, 1856
Photo: Holmes Garden Photos /
Alamy Stock Photo

p.106
Northern rose window of
Chartres Cathedral, France. c.1235
Photo: Guillaume Piolle /
Wikimedia

The School of Life is dedicated to developing emotional intelligence – believing that a range of our most persistent problems are created by a lack of self-understanding, compassion and communication. We operate from ten physical campuses around the world, including London, Amsterdam, Seoul and Melbourne. We produce films, run classes, offer therapy and make a range of psychological products. **The School of Life Press** publishes books on the most important issues of emotional life. Our titles are designed to entertain, educate, console and transform.

THESCHOOLOFLIFE.COM